snow formations

SNOW formations

CAROLYN MARIE SOUAID

George Amabile, Editor

EDITIONS

Cover design by Doowah Design.
Photo of Carolyn Marie Souaid by Mechel Gagnon.

Acknowledgements
The author thanks the Canada Council for the Arts for a grant which provided the time to write. Thanks also to Vivian Trudeau for her thoughtful reading, and to George Amabile for coaxing out the final draft.

Earlier versions of some of the poems were produced by Alison Moss in Toronto for the CBC-Radio series "Home and Away" and broadcast on *Between the Covers* on April 15, 2001.

The poem 'Teacher Gives Hazy Account' is loosely based on a newspaper item which appeared in *The Montreal Gazette* in January 2002.

We acknowledge the support of The Canada Council for the Arts and the Manitoba Arts Council for our publishing program.

Printed and bound in Canada by AGMV Marquis.

National Library of Canada Cataloguing in Publication

Souaid, Carolyn Marie, 1959–
        Snow formations / Carolyn Marie Souaid
Poems.
ISBN 0-921833-85-7

                1. Inuit--Quebec (Province)—Nunavik—Poetry.
I. Title.

PS8587.O87S66 2002   C811'.54   C2002-904512-6
PR9100.3.S585S66 2002

Signature Editions, P.O. Box 206, RPO Corydon, Winnipeg, Manitoba, R3M 3S7

for my mother and father

CONTENTS

I — SOUTH OF THE TREELINE

The Trouble with Being Dead	11
Tabula Rasa	12
Threads	13
Teacher Gives Hazy Account	14
Urban Legend	15
Modern Times	16
Hunger: An Equation	17
Still Life	18
Small Town	19
Running	20
Goodbye	21
Indian Summer	22
Behind the Reflection	23

II — SEDNA, AN INUIT MYTH (APPROPRIATED)

Genesis	27
Maiden	28
Dog-Child (1)	29
Dog-Child (2)	30
Plumbing the Depths	31
Stars	32
Sedna, Revised	33
Evening with the Shaman	34
Sedna, Once-Removed	36
Aboriginal Art	37
Two Reincarnations	38

III — SNOW FORMATIONS

Self Portrait (A Collective Memory)	41
Symposium	42
Archives	43
Arctic Flight	44
Baggage	45
Hands	46
Powerhouse	47

Memory: Autumn   48
Cabin Fever (1)   49
Dinner at Annie's   50
The Elder   52
Artifacts   53
Elisapie   54
Stranded   55
Survival   56
Postcard Home, Delirium   58
Cabin Fever (2)   59
Blind Spot   60
The Student   61
Snow Formations   69
Inukshuk   70
Journal Entry   71
A Closer Look   72
Gestation: Soapstone Carving   74
Falling   75
The Return   76
Solstice   77
Twilight   78
Stonecarver   79
Ice: Break-up   80
The Wind, Not Nothing   81
Mirror Image   82
The Airstrip   83

IV — SOUTH OF THE TREELINE, 2

Coming Home   87
Two Women, Two Salads   88
Sunrise   89
Throat Song   90
Solitude   91
Memento   92
Canvas   93
Still, Life   94

A WORD ABOUT SEDNA

                                        95

The greatest poverty is not to live in the physical world.
                                                    —Wallace Stevens

I

SOUTH OF THE TREELINE

The Trouble with Being Dead

It's the ones walking around you have to worry about.
All flash and strut, but no
heart. Dried-up corn for eyes.
Those dead sleep a long time, midnight stuffing
its black straw into their skulls.

Any one of them will tell you the same thing:
Life falls away in blotches, whole bits at a time
blanking out, like a puzzle
unpiecing itself. Withering into a prairie
for scarecrows, tattered half-men with nothing to do
but scratch around the blueless dark.

And if they'd chosen another path?
Sunnier and more passionate. An ear for the inner voices
talking to them, the tingling air
along the spine.

        Just for a moment, imagine
giving in to your lust, your sequined pangs.
Joy. Acute jags of glass in the wrist.

The trouble with being dead is what you miss:
tin-cold lakewater. The cashmere feel
of a last blurt of blood down the chin.
What you end up settling for: life
as a balance sheet, friends who are either
assets or liabilities.

How that peony in a jar of water
might as well be the wad of fuzz in a senile brain.

For all the impact it has.

TABULA RASA

What if, before he went to pot, Man slipped
into the lab and cleverly cloned himself?
His anachronisms.
Had we only thought ahead.

Had we predicted the swaggering Makers
of laptops and cell phones, the serpentine machinery
of child care.

Had we only anticipated the shark holes
in the ozone, the dirty litter
of stars.

Our tactical human errors.

What if, centuries back, a second cell had emerged
from the boiled waters like frogspawn,
watching over the future?
Some amorphous, swampy blob
only brainier, more discriminating.

Would it have spared us?

Threads

The danger is not what you know
but what you think you know.

Someone famous said that or a fairy
fed it to me in a dream. Either way

the grenade I saw yesterday
on television might have been an artichoke.

And soft green words
might be a figment of your imagination.

Take that couple over there, in the half-light
of an evening tree.

Couldn't the man be mistaken? Couldn't her whispers
in his ear be the trickery of breezes and summer cottons?

Isn't it possible that the elm is really a flimsy
umbrella—

worse, the rain-soaked photo of a flimsy umbrella
coming apart in threads?

Chaos enters the brain swimmingly. Mere humans,
we realign ourselves, posturing.

Teacher Gives Hazy Account

I will not apologize for telling her story. Having followed her around
in the headlines. Having tolerated months of public scrutiny, hordes of
winter trees knocking around
their half-truths. "Absolute morality" branching

into every walk of life. The Protestant ethic.

Seasons passed, eventfully:
I was lonely and happy for the company of teens.
If he were older, we would have been a couple.

Every day, for weeks, she zipped up her long suede boots and strode,
braless, into school. Pushing aside even the air to get to her boys.
"Drunken sex in alleyways and on park benches"
is what the papers said. Every derelict fact exposed: sky
arching its nude back, the liquored sun. Tabloids aside,

let me, for a moment, play Devil's Advocate:
How many of you honestly can't fathom
abandoning yourself to the first betrayal— a slight breeze
through the bedroom window (He who casts the first stone),
whispering into every crack and orifice of your body,
your (loved) one asleep beside you, deep in the crevice
of a dream. Picture it: the slow unleashing of dawn.
Your impulse to leap, irrationally.

Call it "balance," call it the other side, see where it leads you.
The air laced with Jack Daniel's.
Look up "scandal"
in the dictionary, but don't believe everything
you read—
"Relations with a student."
"A not-so-innocent liaison."

Check the footnote down the page, that indiscriminate smear
of ink, bearing your name.

urban Legend

Who, in this hammering heat, has the strength to rape
every last tree in his yard?

What man wields a big brute axe
just to purge nature
of its evil toxins? Industrious,
my foot.

Neighbours like that should be shot. Neighbours like that
deserve to pay

more for their organic greens.

The town's a furnace. Shade is scarce.
For days, I've been holding a fly swatter
over my head.

Someone said he saw a halo
following me around.

modern times

Light-years after the Industrial Revolution
and where has it got me? I'm still here in a bland room
watching reruns of *Gilligan's Island.*
Everything is old hat, including the spiel
of the poor sod I'm about to hang up on.

For a song, he'll rewire my house. I recognize the buzz
in his voice, that radioactive twang.
Meanwhile my attic is jumping
with electricity.

Since when did Hollywood become our Religion?
Who decided we had to sell ice to the Eskimos
when all they ever wanted was to suck back
a candy-red popsicle?

If you really want to know, I own three chairs
and a sideboard I don't even need.
Make that three chairs, a sideboard, and a bedroom set.
All pure mahogany.

     Someone get me out of myself—

what I want more than life
itself
is to taste the genuine
licorice of night!

And if one day you see my face
pressed up against your rainy window,
just think of me as a simple star,
its single, resolute light streaming
down from the empty sky.

Hunger: An Equation

True, it's been simpler dealing with you
out of context: I turned against you,

then turned your grief into an abstraction,
like the theoretical toy
in a Christmas basket, equivalent
to Jello or a coffee bean.
Pleasure for a mirthless boy.

Our last date at Peel and Ste-Catherine
was unlikely as the Garden of Eden or the hypothetical apple.
You busking for quarters, me hugging what agreed
to keep me warm, mostly the blanket.
We ate peanut butter that day
lining our tongues by the spoonful.

The fortification is significant. *Because the scenic factors— trees
starved for leaves, our famished mouths,
the passersby, including their pets, all in scarves—
added up to a great big meaningful
zero.*

All day, our guitar case sat like a neglected kidney
on the sidewalk, the satin insides flapping. Meanwhile,
another variable mucking the odds: swank
at the hotels. The rich wadded in furs,
stepping out of cars. Stepping
out to lunch.

Clearly, extrapolating, we'd be living
on peanut butter the rest of our lives.

still life

I can hardly stand to look
at myself.

What's more horrid is the molten
fruit on the table.

Two mushed lobes
in a bowl.

Skins purpled with
leprosy.

Today, even my brain
has a bad smell.

smaLL town

Father stepped on the gas.
Someone in the back seat was hungry.
Me or my brother. Mom read signs.

Farmer's Daughter. Two miles.
Come and take your pleasure.

We rode the sallow light into town,
acres thick with two-headed corn.
My mouth hanging.

An idiot dog slavered after us, lazy tongue slapping
along the pavement. A second child was starving.

Mom, like a kid herself, breathless —
Ten summers your granddad brought me here!
We stepped on the gas.

Downwind, the carnival was letting out.
Or Sunday Mass.

Everyone on the lawn
had that same dubious gene. Even
the pastor looked a little off.

From there, the road snaked; the insipid trees
degenerated into stumps.

Finally, food. We savoured
the view: more gas-bar than diner.

Closer to something used and discarded:
a condom, a limp mattress.

Mom snapped
her big mouth shut.

We stepped on the gas.

Running

Pushing forty, she wonders how it happened
so fast:

the convoluted skyline, rivers rushing double-time
to energize the night.

Didn't we just yesterday climb down from the trees?

Somewhere en route, adolescence, the world sprang
out of hand. Fluorescents surged, shocking

pupils, pinkish lab-rats, out of amnesia.
A teacher leapt at the board, acrobatic
with his numbers.

Meanwhile, outside, it was November, skeletal, a labyrinth
of wires and crossed branches.

Her mind raced in a hundred directions:
sex, hair, sex, clothes, sex, lipstick
husband, car, house, dog.

Running, she knew there was no going back.
Through the veined pathways

of the frosted window, she glimpsed
the primary school emptying out across the street,
children trudging home
to their aproned mothers
powdered in flour,

the weekly pot
of stew, simmering.

Goodbye

for Gérard Blua

No one stopped me when I left.
No one cursed the sky or penned an epic.
No one shouted: *By God, it's the end of the world!*

But wait— what was *that* at the hotel?
That one bright stop in your arms
before the night washed me away.
What was that thing I felt in place of your heart?
The void, the zero, the rumbling absence.
The shudder. The bomb-blast.

The vast
imploded planet.

Actually, the world didn't end. No one cut off an ear.

You wore your beard long that fall
and shaggy. Outside was red and wet and
kissed with leaves. You hugged me.

Just like that.

I wanted to say *yes, yes.* I was just noticing how
the doors had parted like lovers, like continents,
I'd been meaning to tell you that

while the rain fell around us
in dribs and drabs.

indian summer

The frail red leaves took a stand.
No more scratching the surface. No
more small talk. The shuttered house
is not for sale. Nor are the contents:
permanent fixtures, upright piano.

The hopeful few within, their shelled
hearts like fists. The hard nut
of winter is coming

    — crack it!

Behind the Reflection

See for yourself—

roll your rational eye backwards into the
brainless dark

stare at the glass, stare until the soupy swamp
dampens your gaze and disarms you

bog for days, eons

let the great spear of light
fork down on the fluid world, draining it
to salt

see her slowly take root among the primates
upright, cutthroat, woman
in her cave-paint hugging the first bone tool

look carefully, open your heart to her

      —she is you

II

SEDNA, AN INUIT MYTH
(APPROPRIATED)

Genesis

You arrived like a gift
in darkest January,
small white fire
burning in a bleak tent,
mesmerizing the cold, the hunger,
the miserable constellations.

The curious wandered into your
perfect light,

eyes seething like stars.

No one knew how long it would last, or
what lay at the core of your glow.
Only that there were flashes of blue
amid the flames. Illusion or not,
it was day again.

Who knew that the heat you spread
across their faces, those clever shadows
would soon beget a larger,
more barbaric hell,
a vile stretch of death and night,
death and fornication, death and starvation

      —and death again.

maiden

Ripening dawn. Your father's exposed legs
across the bed, deified.

You won't go, though he prods you gently
with the lip of his toe. Leaves you
wondering

in the ambivalent light.
What man nudges you out, clothes you,
moistens your mouth for another? What father recoils,
cowardly, from your own new breasts, furtive
little dormice stirring
beneath the sheets?

The only crude thing is the day
shaping up outside: rotting animal skins,
thawed moraines of garbage.

Like all your days ahead, prophesied
in his half-hearted talk of the necessary
suitors,
those who will feed you
the sordid, unalterable truth, entering
and re-entering you, reveling
as you rub up against the dirty
linen of the world.

Dog-child (1)

Your father sold you to his wolf-dog
who humped you raw; later, the bloodied mess
blackened around your bastards.
Our rough pink tongues licked you dry,
toughening you up
while the sea darkened
around your rapist, our father,

sucked him down
like a stone.

Don't forget me—I'm the one you banished
to the South, wilderness
of grit and steel. I am the White girl
pacing the streets, talking to myself
while my brothers breathe the good
salt air.

Dog-child (2)

Sea Goddess, Mother,
you were mine first, I feel it
in my loin, every mated cell of you,
your human blood,

how my father dangled his lank bone
until it hardened and infiltrated
your prim scent. Suckle me, Mother,
drag me, thrashing, onto the snow-scuffed
earth, train me to beg and bite and claw
and kill and worship the flesh.

Watch me die and
die again; watch me,
I will return, stronger
than you.

Plumbing the Depths

You who have known malice in the human heart:
a man rowing gently into the carmine light,
away from you, knowingly,
as vultures darken the side of your boat,
baiting the sharks
with their scrawny flesh.

You who have known worse: your own father
raising his oar against you, smashing your knuckles,
until your hands, hands of his hands,
sever under the blows. You, whose hacked-off fingers
floated like wreckage to the ocean floor
while the aberrant moon tossed in its sleep.
You, who have sunken into your cold lair,
salivating, as the bloated stubs comb the sand
for a last grab at life.

stars

A little perspective on the frantic boat
and those spook hands pawing the air—
the stars willed it; they condoned it.
Like Shakespeare masterminding a plague
on your house. Or Satan threading a tapeworm
through the sleeping brain.

The sky always has its way of
shuffling the Big Deck.

Those same stars put me in SoHo one night,
understated light
tingeing the veiled room mauve.

The air was moist with predictions.
A gypsy said *You are an old soul*,
meaning this was my last time around.

Meaning I'd definitely been here before.
My sweating palms made stars.

Helplessly, the cards fluttered through her fingers
before the Queen of Spades settled on top,
the inescapable, black point arrowing
down. And in that flash,
my sinking heart saw a desperate figure
rippling like a frond under water, diminished
by fear and praying
for her life to reconvene—

     her severed joints to reconfigure
as the mighty fish of the sea.

sedna, revised

One by one, you swallowed
the rotted-out boats,
gobbled them whole
like babies.

Underwater, your eyes decayed,
your brain turned black. Your hair
tangled with the plants
and snaked
across emptiness.

Cold-blooded mermaid,
what if this were your story:

What if nature had delayed
your curved hips, the inevitable
fleshing-out of sex?

Picture *terra firma*, your new life:
thighs crayoned pink, the dormant pearl
still snugly in place.

Running, you flee the wolves in your skirt,
the blushing hillside,

the sun, whose scandalous light
will leave you cold.

evening with the shaman

Expecting him, she does laundry.
Dusts the furniture. Stocks her fridge
with a case of beer.
Just what does he think, the rat.
I'll let him off easy?

She pumices the dead skin,
rouges her mouth.

A little leg would be good.
She hauls out her best black stockings,
sheer with a seam up the back. Paints
her toenails alternately blue and green.
Seaweed tones to match the walls.

Dims the lights. Jazzes up the place
with a little Coltrane.

He arrives at nine on the button,
lusting after her hair. This guy with a history.
No hello, how's the weather, no kiss my ass, no nothing.
Sizing her up, fantasizing, he sees meat and only meat.
Her layered red cache.

She disengages, biting her tongue.
Gently, slyly, makes an offering:
celery in a dish. A crisp heart
of lettuce.

The louse is getting nowhere,
and he knows it. Tries reverse
psychology,
doctoring his words—
Hey, Baby.

Egg in the face.
A cold turnip.

Her monstrous hair dissolves
into snakes.
Wrapping around him.

He senses an iceberg in the cards.
Calamity. Another millennium
of dearth.

Go, girl.

*From now on, Buster, it'll be nothing
but slim pickings.*

sedna, once-removed

Everything is seduction.
The way to understand a metaphor
is to undress her, coyly.
Bit by bit.

On the cabaret table, a hint
of snow: one white candle, tapered.
Spilled salt on a red cloth.
Pellegrino, bottled at source (Italy).

The businessman softens
his young virgin.

Reading the wine card
like someone with his hands
on a rare piece of art.

Study those last lines.
Are they suggestive enough for you?

You should have read:
"The crowded room melting away.
People misting and evaporating—
their delicate erasure."

You should have read: "Her pearling strip of satin."

You should have pictured
        groundlessness, weightlessness,

an elegant fan, perhaps
turning

a slow, deliberate,
circular wind.

Aboriginal Art

At the height
of the market,
in its heyday,
a thousand bucks
could buy you
a spot in the
warm-paneled interiors
of the rich

next to

a silver candlestick,
3 pewter jugs,
and a bronzed
hubcap.

Backs turned,
the cars are barely a memory.

two reincarnations

1.

Winter paws the room white.
Your shy self, once-removed,
strays in.
Sheepishly.

Whose January are you?

Whose unshackled sky?

2.

Don't underestimate the subtlety
of snow. Winter shocks the clenched mind,
dislocating neurons.

Note how the merest hole in a cloud
becomes a gateway, a door.

How one simple flake
triggers an entire blizzard.

All those years of unremembered light
avalanching through a crack.

And just yesterday
I had the world figured out.

III

SNOW FORMATIONS

seLf portrait (a coLLective memory)

I don't care, you said,
nude and gleaming
in the aquarium glow of water.
You filled the tub, you and your yellow ducks.
The ocean rose to your chin. Clearly,
the photographer was smitten with you—
firstborn,
precocious, a subject beyond perfection.
But can we excuse him? Isn't *he* somehow accountable
for your haughty reflection, your ruthless toe
stirring up the tide, upending
the snowy bar of soap?

Can a man be so wrapped up in his art
that he doesn't notice a wayward floe
and its deathbound tribe,
turbulence making seaspray
of their soft goodbyes?

symposium

We handed them God on a silver platter.
Do you know it took Him only one day to annihilate
the past? Which, of course, allowed them
to start over again.

     In a flash,

He gave them light and a place to gather:
Pool halls and greasy shacks.
The world sugared white.

We took up the slack.

Served up their heart's desire: Export A
and an excuse to get up in the morning.
Vinegar on fries. Cameras to seize the day:

Dogs coveting cigarette butts,
An elder's rotten keyboard of teeth.

We gave them mercantile lust
and the cunning
to turn 4,000 savage years
into art.

See that sky up there? That was us, too.

We gave them television,
liberalism, tampons, Pampers,
Pop Tarts, tooth paste, acne, tartrazine.
Did I mention Sugar Pops? Xanthan gum,
Hubba Bubba, Boy George,
Ringo, Paul, John, and Love, all they needed.
With protection (which, of course, they still won't use).
The rest just came: Woodstock, Hollywood, the World
Wide Web.

The nerve of them saying we stole their land.
Such a small thing.

archives

*Greer
.Poem*

The first step in liquidating a people is to erase its memory.
— Milan Hubl

We were lofty: just look at the facts.

For eons, the blank sky sprawled.
Then, that fledgling plane
pushed into view.

A clump of Eskimos dotted the airstrip,
their raw, prehistoric faces
fending off a storm.

The priest arrived in his Catholic dress,
young and earnest and hungry for schools.
His pious robes blackened the portal
of the boys' dorm while a candle burned slyly
in his hand. Its long, erect wick forcing
upward in the cold.
The years came

and went. Someone down south fathered
a dream. Governments came

and went. More dreams. Doctors and nurses
and do-gooders sifting in with the wind—
planeloads of them, eager
to crank the huge gears
of civilization.

As if their smart, white machines
could reinvent the snow.

Arctic Flight

January limped in like an old crone:
haggard snow, a weak pulse
of sky through the skinny trees.

All last fall, the graveyard leached
into the water table. Leaves wallowed
in their own waste. Soon,
even the birds were spent.

I myself flew
into exile—

way north of the trees
with a knapsack, and a bottle of brandy
buried in my eiderdown coat

stared from the small plane
as my fissured, brown
liver-spotted town
vaporized in the dark air

and when I woke, the world had accumulated again
outside my window

the strapping, white, freshness of it
shoveling life
back into my eyes.

Baggage

The world is slower and duller than I thought.
And those traveling pockets of excitement in the sky,
ribbons and party bags, are nothing

but clouds. Did you know the Inuit have no words
for "forecast" and "certainty"?
I might have dreamt that.

I've had plenty of time to sleep.

What I know: each day
stiffens another crust of bread.
Count on nothing.

Count back to zero.

five, four, three

Think: warm water, chamomile.

two

Think: slow
Himalayan climb.

one, zero—
serenity.

I wait for my things to arrive, rationing
patience, raisins,

country
(yawn)
& western.

Hands

The box arrived on a Tuesday, the omnipotent
Queen on every stamp.
I remember it well because afterwards,
things were never the same: my hands.

Picture the impoverished landscape, the poorest
of soil. And then a package filled with the garish fruit
of September:

eggplant, pomegranate. A surfeit
of plums. Enough to feed a small continent

      —but, I exaggerate. Not having been myself that day.

Startled by a mouse hidden in among the apples,
blinking up at me in terror.

Creatures, we eyeballed, ready to lunge.

What followed: nocturnal rumblings, the room
blurring and dissolving, the house.

And then, something like light passing between us,
bathing us in its sheen: instinct, foreboding.

Brick by brick, the walls resurrected.
My couch, where he burrowed, fearful.

The clock, chiming, resumed its normal hour,
but by the time

I grabbed whatever thing I could
to stake him out—yardstick, skewer—
my wildcat hands
had already pounced.

The pummeled rind of him still
squirming
      long after his heart gave out.

powerhouse

Bear-fisted Jimmy's soused again
drawling sweat from his jaw
pawing the room
in a primitive light.
Bam.
My stupid refrigerator gets in his way
and he threatens to knock
its sorry white face
from here to Iqaluit.

*great
description*

You'd think that at
six-foot four
all that sludge and sewage
surging through him
like blood
    he'd be a big guy—

when the hockey game's done, he wants
insists
on having him some woman.

I defer, he packs the knife.

(CODA)

Jimmy's brain is nothing
but water sloshing around
the cold steel bowl of his skull.

Ribboning to the floor,
his damp white shirt a wash of surrender,
he floats off to sleep
until the abrupt noise
of his own fart startles him to life.
Laughter and tears
muddle like snot.

    Seven years later, he cocks a .22 and blows the ocean
through his ears.

memory: autumn

What to make of the landscape, the sudden
depletion: shorter, colder days. Not a single tree
to wave goodbye to. Uprooted,

the fugitive geese in some other sky.

Home, being different, there were nuances.
Death I understood as a continuum
of events:

the sun fizzling out in increments,
people buttoned into woolens and cardigans.
Gathering up logs.

Year in, year out: a gradual tapering. Heat softly storing itself
in another part of the globe.

The ritual passage: anxiety. Roads sponged with leaves.
A carload of elderly aunts for dinner.

Hideous as prunes, they sat with us by the fire,
their gnarled shadows scaling the walls,
imperceptibly.

Children, we focused on the ticking hands
of the clock, the dwindling coals, those women

like hags at the cauldron
hoarding the last pumpkin hours.

cabin fever (1)

It was me, myself, in the mirror.
It was the empty wine glass on the table.
And the curtained window, like a drawstring
on the world. It was the dogless
horizon, the recurring spaces between clouds.
It was the gale force, ripping through
colour, salmon and cerulean flattened
into monotones. It was the grey void of water,
the one wrong step to certain death. It was the frozen
membrane starting up again, the coming dread—
next week, next month, the cold shoulder
of snow against the door, the house,
the entire hamlet. It was what I was waiting for,
what would never come, something, anything
to neutralize the chill. It was thoughts of my mother
in a spring dress, days behind in her correspondence.
All her drawers of empty blue envelopes.
It was footprints, receding; their zeroes
growing fainter and fainter.

    It was me, myself, in the mirror.

Dinner at Annie's *I love this poem*

I mouth them with a pure heart,
smackingly— *musk-ox, caribou.*
Others, too.
Lemming.

Do you know how much life slips away
uncatalogued each day? How many words.
Warm clot of mother's milk.
     I didn't mean words, I meant heft.
The sinewed world.

How did my convoluted journey
get me here? Guest in a strange home.

     A tool on page nine of *Getting to Know
the North* arrives in my hand. Moonshaped,
for cutting.

Observant, they would have caught me
gloating. Schooled in such trivia.

Need I remind you how the brain responds?

Involuntarily, and with passion.
Conspiring, as always, with the tongue.
Having learned an expression
or two. Simple nouns.
Ulu.

Did no one hear me?

Tuktumik takuvunga.

An eye turns. Another turns
into the light, checking a toenail. Concurrently,

dinner opens up on the floor, rations on the tough hide
of a box slit along the seams. The rest is all basic
vocabulary: kneel, gnaw, scrape, slurp.
Bodily stuff. Punctuated by silence.
Fart. Burp.

Long story short: a good table. Animal parts
shorn and tossed, a slurry
of bones and fat.

Deep in the small of my back,
vibrations from the next room.
Someone's brambly throat
headed for a clearing.

As though a voice were on the way.

The Elder

There's a story we like to tell.
The one about the old woman sewing cross-legged
on her plywood floor, her forehead rutted and textured
as a walrus. The woman is generic.
She is any one of them. See how she squints long and hard
into the eye of her needle,
as though she were looking for a way out
of her predicament?

The first time she saw a plane, she chased it
with her father's gun
but that shiny, unnatural bird shot through the sky
like no ptarmigan she'd ever seen.

In the blink of an eye, her world became a scrapyard
of sheds and government houses, of streets
leading nowhere, of TV sets flashing
diaper ads and soap operas at unsuspecting children.
Night piled up over the dirty snow.
A motley pack of dogs darkened the village.

Study her carefully: old brown woman in mukluks
and mismatched clothes embellishing the days
with colourful yarn.
See how her hand pushes back tired wisps
of hair from her face, how she positions
the large rusty blades of her scissors
on either side of the thread,
checking and double-checking her work
before making the next snip. See how her eyes cloud over
when she remembers she is doing it all for money
        —another artifact for another white tourist.

Outside her window, it is always the same
plodding horizon. If this is *her* story,
how can *I* tell it?

How to write the fleeting moment, the look in her eye,
the shadow of better times? Who, but she
can recall her younger self in the midnight sun
pattering after an Arctic tern?

Artifacts

Assorted broken dolls
by a gravesite,
armless, nude,
eyes obliterated
by centuries of ice.

One might confound them
with those running
wounded
from their men:

Eskimo wives
in southern dress,
bandaged
in the stubborn moss
of June.

Don't.

ᴇʟisapie

Every day a little more truth welled up inside her.
As though, somehow, she saw the big picture.

At school, her fingers made bottomless pools,
the thin, white page swimming with paint, unable to absorb
her dappled imagination.

She spent all six years of her life measuring
pigments and light, waiting
for just the right conditions.

Finally, the geese darted into black formation.
An unstable boat waited expectantly.

Legend has it she went down smiling
as the lake closed its cold mouth
over her head.

It was her finest work. She drew water
into her lungs as the sky floated off in its garbled light,
as she sank deeper and deeper into the avant-garde,
the most incredible thoughts flooding in—
generations of dead elders,
every last child of the North, her brother
who never got past the salted womb,

waiting for her
in a grain of sand.

stranded

Someone miscalculated the day.
      Or purposely put us to the Test.

Gave us one measly boat to defend ourselves
against those conniving rocks, slicing through the rapids
like fins. We saved ourselves and camp floated in
on a risky patch of land

just as the miserable clouds
netted the last of our light.

Days we were stuck there with nothing to do
but count the accidents
of nature,

the number of blueberry stains on our hands, and how many times
a day we rinsed out the same tin cup. We counted
our steps to the pee-hole, our steps
from here to there—to drinking water so cold
it seared our hands.

Mostly, we shivered in the damp tent
as the weather collapsed around us.

That's when we began to hallucinate— saw God's mean face
in a thundercloud, literally caught his fickle hand
pouring a flask of rain all over us.
We watched our guides empty the rum,
watched the storm bulge up
inside them, their savage bodies crossing the line
into roaring madness, floundering hell,
on and on and on
until finally misplacing themselves
in a big senseless heap on the floor.

At dawn, we awoke to the volatile sun.

survivaL

Coolly is how woman dispenses life
to the man, how she discreetly
withholds.

Invoking the glacial geology
of her brain.

As you begin to envision "reprisal" or
a settling of accounts, picture the harsh relief
of ice outside, herds disappearing. A hunter,
for good measure,
facing off with Sedna.

The adversity is unspoken, though not benign.
Historically, it isn't in him to beg
that times be softer, more accommodating.
What he understands: the vicious wind
in his face could last years.

At the breathing hole, he waits
for a sign,
life, movement, anything.
The full moon a succulent dish overhead.
Like bannock, alluring.
Suppose he is your husband.

Suppose it is another century.
A mysterious, dark-haired stranger entices him
for a drink. She is wearing something
low-cut and red. She is not a bad person,
though some might speculate.
For several hours, she bends his ear.

Meanwhile, in an unheated apartment across town
your own ears are burning.
The kids you made with this man are crying.
Never mind crying, they are bawling.
None of you has eaten in days.

To survive, you huddle with them in one place,
the bed, for example,
gathering everyone into your quilted darkness.

Like fish you'd swallow, whole.
As you've guessed, this is not really a story

        of vengeance,
it is one of circumstance,
how the world survives
despite the cruel coupling
of events.

Today you eat sparingly, tomorrow you gorge.
Your man crawling in beside you

and on his breath,
the warm scent of meat.

postcard home, delirium

Anyone sane would ask the question.
What's a choppy 8-millimeter film doing outside
my window? And who are those windblown actors
flying across my screen, sped-up, grainy,
clutching one another for dear life?

The phones are dead, so I'm writing you this
huddled against a lantern with my flask
of Southern Comfort. Listen.
Can you hear it?

Flapping celluloid. The crinkled
minus-60 air.

Trust me. This is no bit part, it's the role of a lifetime:
mummy in a sleeping bag,
staving off the chill.

Never mind.

I could have been an ice cube
or a solitary flake. Blue-breath frost
on the earth's white brain.

Haven't seen the sun in months.
Wish you (it) were here.

cabin fever (2)

Outside, flustered snow
caught in a criss-crossing wind.

Every night, the same tune. Stereo playing
its slow saxophone
for my drowsing mug of gin.

Lamplight's languid glow
on the walls.

My orange cat in a half-moon
licking itself to sleep. Or—

snapshot of

my orange cat in a half-moon
licking itself to sleep.

The record is

skipping. None of us is
going anywhere.

Down south,
      it's spring.

Blind spot

Logic? It kept me going for years, watching
over me, rescuing me from the uncertain dark.
Who dared question the sanity
of eating and sleeping?
The planets were predictable.
I was a kept woman.

A voice warned me. The Killer Bees
came and went, baffling
governments for all of a day.
We tolerated estrogen in the tap water,
a hundred years of soot in our lungs.
A boy down the street grew
a third eye.

      Last night, walking, I heard the voice again.

It spoke the emptiness of the grave, turned the world
inside out. I floundered in its blind spot.

Hudson Bay, black, terrifying,
trailed me like the cold night-breath
of dogs.

I tried staying focused, a straight line the smartest path
between two points. But what were those shifting shadows
gathering around me,

those nervous pairs of eyes?

The student

1.

Every day the words freeze in your throat
but, still, you go on
surprising me.
Tell me, what are you scribbling
there in the rough cloth
pages of your book?

Today, the sky's a joy: plush
velour, texture I can really sink my teeth into.
Not like the other sky I left behind:
drab sheets of metal
nailed over cities and electric pylons.

It's taken time, but I'm getting used to the
long, empty silences,
the rugged lines. The way, each day,
you force open my eyes a little more.

Your note addressed "to teacher"
floats into my hands,

an unnerving puzzle
of white space.

There, buried in the deep snow,
the palest of footprints.

Nature doesn't fail, you wrote.
People fail.

2.

Sixty-three words for "snow"
and still I don't know
what to call the thin, feathered kind:
tremors on the roof.

From home, I watch you
on your sled, strapping gear.
Young, bare hands like those of a man
working the rough, white
grain of the ice.

A small wind blows up the staircase
of my spine—

a sign

and soon we are beyond the hills,
gorging on cloud and air, billowing

through voluptuous drifts
of meringue.

3.

Back home, we'd have called it a date—
the way you came for me in your baseball cap,
cigarette jammed behind an ear;
the way we made tracks on your sled
like lovers on the run;
the way the copper light rounded
our huddled shapes
hounding us
through the clapping cold.

4.

You load up the rifle, alerted
to a change in the land, an unmistakable wind.
Abandon me to the desert
of my youth—

humdrum memories of the countryside.
Mom in her straw hat, pointing out the cows.
Annotating every trivial tree.
Dad cutting the motor so we can all coast
through that Indian afternoon.
Heat swelling up the back seat,
while the inconsequential world
drones past.

Elsewhere on the planet,
people are with people.

My shadow reaches across the snow
like a long blue arm
but already you are a waning speck
in the scheme of things, expendable
vertebrate in the food chain.

And if you don't come back,
what then?

5.

Your gun startles the snow
into a soft, white commotion.

At the tail end of silence,
the shuddering mass and
its burgeoning red stain.

We are all three in our own state
of madness.

Soon, a flurry
of voices in my head.

Urging me over impossible roads
to where you are no longer boy
but hero, predator, any man
who will lead me into the naked wilderness
of his breast.

Best not complicate a thought:

far away, you kneel in a thatch of blood,
fingers in mouth, throat sucking down
the livery bits of your kill.

Your gun startled me—
a blizzard, then nothing
but the simple light and
your solitary figure
humbling itself
to the sky.

6.

What it means to be
vulnerable:

two snowflakes
on this immense, white planet.

Riding home behind you,
my body exposed
like a bare nerve.

Your young, human back
dishing out warmth.

17, and already you've fathered a child.
What have I ever done?

Who have I loved?

7.

Civilization is homing in on us.
Your finger points ahead
to the dusky village,

tangerine glow
over a wing of snow.

Time is running out.
We are racing over perilous ice.
The wind scrambling my hair
is from hell.

8.

Tilting my head
in the coarse light

the horizon is a strand
of your hair

a long mysterious stretch
of darkness. I reach up to touch
the end of the world.

It is not so daunting.

snow formations

Pale light drifts
over puffs of snow

tugging at the eye,
the sleepy heart.

Your hand travels
into mine,

tracing every line
and curve.

Even in death there is life,
you say.

Listen to the way   *silence*

fills up with   *silence*

;

listen to the dunes

:

they are talking to you.

inukshuk

That brown speck on the tundra
that thing like lint
on a white dress,
that's me.
Move a little closer.

Seems I've been here since the Vikings,
since way before you.
For years, I've watched the herds
come and go. The river.

I can certainly tell you a little something
about bearing up, stalwart. Resilient.
Unaffected by the rose moss
springing in a breeze,

the teardrop
clouds.

Let me tell you about the stone
will. How, even through the
poignant light of softer days
I go on, standing.
Visibly intact. Touch me,
and I fall apart.

journal entry

Naming it "the best day of my life"
I was recalling the trapped wind in my boots,
my ballooning hood. The prudish white moon
spying down on us from the sky.

I wanted to record the drama in my heart, my head,
winged burst of light, the *whorling*. I wanted

you, no—

I wanted language, Orwellian precision.
The words *spiral, concentric, ringed*
pelvic heat.

I wrote and wrote, grabbed challenge

by the throat, wanting it all
on paper, frozen,

a moment in time, exactly:

fresh dung on the snow, curled heap
of earth and steam;

my lips and tongue rounding your fingers,
oil, blood,

the snared fox in my mouth,
dithering.

A CLOSER LOOK

(SCENE)
Igloos facing in on each other.
You and I, sheltered in one.
Feeding on equal strands
of meat.

Several days

you don't talk, even
when passing me the tea
and your thumb accidentally
grazes my breast,
your suddenly shy eyes flee behind a quiet wall
of hair. No cough, not even a clearing
of the throat.

Earlier, a close call on dangerous ice. My quickened heart
speaking for both of us. I fell,
artfully, into your arms.

(SEEN)
City girl's big breast
brassing up the peace

the whole honky-tonk world
twinging and twanging
from her pores

sugar, booze, cars

a crazed highway
horning in on, mussing up
dizzying
the innocent bystander.

(DECONSTRUCTED)
The second igloo is moot. Also, the vitriolic airs
of the watchful tribe. Further possibilities:
the boy's own guilty conscience
zooming in on itself; a mere drift of snow
misconstrued due to the sun
casting the wrong sort of glow
on the day.
As in the foreign film *Soleil Trompeur*
where the deceptive *sun* spitefully exposes
the deceptive *son* to his people.

One sees
how easily it can happen.

Gestation: soapstone carving

Nothing in the stone but the ephemeral dance
rippling through time: the swimming
possibilities.

Your fish eye.

Fins and gills. Silvery sparks
of life on the verge.

Shyly, you emerge
in human terms, ambient light
hugging your back, dividing—

until now, there are two of you:

lovers, filling with sand

and drifting along the ocean floor,
phenomenal pressure of the sea
on your lungs.

Your marine ballet wavers—
                    momentarily.

Buoyant, you come up for breath,
your beaded skins glistening.

There is an infant between you.

Graceful choreography
salting the air.

FaLLing

Amnesia or euphoria?
Loss of memory, hence forgetfulness.
Occasioned by amorous folly.

Head's top half blown off,
the heavy sky
        swimming down:

winged cherubs sprinkling diamond rain

the giddy barometer,
falling.

Did I dream your rogue tongue
on my catholic thigh?

That moist disturbance.

The Return

We stood in judgment
beneath the glaring sky, oblivious
to the stars, to the many eyes
of the sloped hills.

The dire warnings of your dead elders,
mounded in snow.

Their ghostly discord poisoned the village:
worse than catcalls, sugar-coated pleasantries.
Everyone shocked by your innocence.

How you didn't even realize the power
of your own body. What I would not do

to accommodate, opening myself up
to the ocean

fluid, unaccountable, as in a dream
where there are no boundaries.
My wanton hair drifting.

All your hand touched was my cheek.

How did we not see the partial light
for what it was: subterfuge, divine
intervention?

Darkness, intruding.

soLstice

Finally, everything out in the open:
our heavy secret, a dark-bellied wine in the glint
of my ring.
The burst grapes leaked
ceremoniously down my chin.

Possibly, and from a great height,
animal blood.

Did I say that the rhythms changed?
That Earth suddenly sped up a notch while
Hades breathed deeply from the night between rocks?
And you, in your hunting clothes, so hot
I could barely touch. We stopped,
willingly.
Savoring the goosebump thrill,
the dilated heart
over the temperate life.

Not tea and oranges for breakfast, or
a whitewashed fence.

Just the restless flesh, cusping.

Twilight

Maybe this, maybe that. Nothing is sure,
not even the salmon
plume of light on the horizon.

Someday, a plane will land. Someday,
my spring boots will punch through the ice.

Someday, the sun will catch up, making furred lines
acute again.

On a rack outside your flimsy house,
a caribou strung out to dry, its future
hanging in the balance.

Like your mom in the shadows of her kitchen,
playing bingo with the radio. Tomorrow, she will beat the hide
into a pair of mitts.

Or, she will let your dad's fist
find every supple bone
in her face.

I want to help her.
You want to kiss me.

The darkening air is a skin
between us.

stonecarver

There is much that happens (between) the time the stone is found
and the time the people in the south see it as a bird or anything.
— *Paulosie Kasadluak*

Not you, but one of you,
is dead. Hours ago,
while the sky was still

green as stone,

a half-dozen fault lines
running through it.

One village north, a chirping
bullet found his head.
Apparently, all she had said,
his white lover, was: *no.*

Striking a raw nerve. Chipping
away at him. He left no note,

no apology. Nothing
(for the Guild of Crafts)

but two sculptures. One on the bureau,
free-form creature
towering into flight;

the second, lifeless on a pillow,

the manna lifted
right out of it.

ice: break-up

We went to the island my last afternoon.
Wore sweaters only, and oversized scarves.

I must have sensed the impossible
drift of that day: river on hind legs, crazed
into sculpture.

Modest wind trembling
through the blown glass.

An odd clinking.

You murmured possibilities: *husband, wife, hunting.*

I said *home.* What I remember most:

how, momentarily, sun and moon
shared the same spring sky. How ice-blue,

yet flushed
the snow appeared.

The wind, not nothing

It's not in the steady pull of light toward you, but in
the first instant, the flash, when suddenly you recognize
the capacity for ugliness and beauty
under one roof. Whitefish. Rusty cigarette foil
floating backwards in the sea. What it all means
for the silvered brain. To harbour interconnectedness:
a man dies and the rest of the world goes on thrashing
someplace else. To see deception in all its prisms: snowflakes
and their glass houses. A loved one, cutting you.
To stare into someone's downcast eyes and still see
summer's compassionate hours: the delicate
browns of flowering mushrooms. Scruff returning
to the fold. Arctic heather. A gull, say, and its wan shadow,
traipsing after the wind.
The wind, I said—not
nothing.

Mirror image

My liquid

dream foretold the end

menstrual sap, sweet
silent resignation

your one green tear

a belly of rain.

The Airstrip

I stare through a small window,
registering your face one last time, your composure
in the violent start-up of the engine,
long black hair flying.

What we both desired—my body
filled with child

—was impossible.
Simplicity.

Tomorrow, the moneyed world will come jangling back
and the bloodsucking banks,
like my relatives,
will all be smiling my way.

Even the ordinary sun
will be issuing orders: eat, sleep, work.

It is blustering madness as we lift away.

Moments later, from the sky,
the turbulent snow is serene again,
tranquil.

You seem to be waving, hushed
blue shadow of the plane
passing over you.

How could I refuse your kiss, the one
gift without any strings attached?

IV

SOUTH OF THE TREELINE, 2

coming Home

You're back after the long haul.
The photographs on the wall are still
stuck in their frames. The family,
all in bed, sleep soundly.
Taking the refrigerator for granted:
foods arranged alphabetically,
measured fists
of cookie dough zipped into bags.

      But hold on—
when it comes right down to it,
who can say with absolute certainty
that at some critical point in time
life didn't fail them, too?
That, for the one moment your back was turned,
another of these bored, unfulfilled souls
didn't just up and blow off
his tepid surroundings.
Didn't just grab the car keys
and ram full speed into the reckless light.

You pause a moment, looking for signs:
five o'clock shadow, furze
on the peppers. A messy spill of salt.
What you see is a first crack
of dawn through the blinds,
the escaping darkness.

The floors are making sounds
you don't recognize.
Every lampshade in the place is
down to dust. The wall
between the den and the hall
is gone.

two women, two salads

How can you? she says. *See a blue day.*
Just that.
It's all in the way she picks
at the mango on her plate, her eyes souring
on the blackish rose in the centrepiece vase.
Glazing over.

In 29 days, 12 hours, and 44 minutes,
the moon will have travelled once around the Earth.
She knows this. She knows

that someone she hasn't met yet will be
arriving regularly.
Leaving a second toothbrush with her, a change
of underwear. That things will insinuate themselves,
insidiously: broadloom, upholstery. A state-of-the-art recliner.
At tax time, his whip-sharp accountant.
That her floorspace will start shrinking,
while those things, multiplying exponentially,
begin to take on a life of their own.
Expanding into concepts.
Bending and curving into every room
of the house, every tuck and crease. And then, the alien factor.
Strangers inhabiting her Rolodex, spinning a little Feng Shui
through her universe. Her kitchen of brushed nickel
looking eerily like outer space, the walls
spackled a greyish dust.

How can you not? I ask, raying my lettuce into
petals of sun.

Thinking of you.

sunrise

This is America; this is not the Middle East.
These are the tiny tremors multiplying silently,
exponentially, in the trenches of your gut.

This is the pale, shirred sky before the rumble
of television. See how it harbours all the good in the world,
all the pent-up rage. Don't expect comfort.

Don't expect a benevolent squeeze on the arm.

The sun is about to fly up out of nowhere,
a shocking red blast that will put all machines,
all technology, to shame. Astonished,
you will call it a sun to end all suns,
this inverted mushroom
of cloud and soot, an entire furnace
collapsing in on itself.

Minutes—no—hours later, you will still be there,
knee-deep in rubble, hair matted down, body fighting
the residue of firedust in your lungs.
And then, you will spot it—

       a tiny miracle, growing

up out of a crack in the sidewalk,
intact, undisturbed— a dandelion.
Gently, careful not to shake it, you will bend down
and pluck it, intricate planet of dust and atoms,
you will bury your cheek in its yellow cushion,
its soft spoked face,

and you will embrace the new day.

Throat song

It was the end of God and abstractions, my last year
in school. Dusk penetrating a shingled
beach house. The suffocating
humidity.

Bedside, a few thin volumes. Beckett and
his dark oeuvre.

      Who knows how it happened, or why—
a mysterious bird arrived on my sill
like so much light,

puffing up his chest,

the raspberry sky
speaking mountains
through him.

Shifting my attention to the salted particulars:
algae, starfish,
the ordinary
granular sea
out there.

Making the wait /
weight bearable.

soLitude ~~incredible~~

Rituals to pass time: pacing
the floor, ironing.

Mine: lighting the stone hearth
with a long match, watching
applewood blaze and curl to ash,

a great civilization
eating itself into char and destruction.
Hours later, Thebes in ruins.

The cooling house.

Admittedly, the physics still shocks me:
how energy, never quite lost, always returns
disguised

the way a lilac reappears
in the winter

sky
as the pulsing Northern Lights.

Grief, what is stored in the heart,
still flares up.

memento

Ten years, and I can't bring myself to destroy
the one mental image I have left,
gritty Polaroid of you grinning
despite time, despite the wife pulsing with child,
the multiple offspring (how many now?),
the house, the sled, the returning
geese, despite the moon, halved and quartered
and finally obliterated, despite summer,
fall, winter, the revolving planets.

Why have I let you go on
arguing the impossible? That life has fixed you
there in that pose, stalled you at 17
by the river where I gave you
my mother's ring, the one I wore
every day, as a keepsake. Already by then,
spring had sheared most of the snow.
Even the static cold was retreating.

Above your head,
caramelized light.

Sweet one, you were no saint.

canvas

In the end, only the beach can speak
for itself. All day, I watched the sun
scald and bleach.

The sky whipped up a storm
of gulls. Shapeless, unassuming,

white is the tufted breath of clouds,
silence, feathering in
where words leave off.

White is effortlessly white.

At dusk, the sea left
its foamy configuration
in the sand.

All day I waited,
but my thoughts would not turn into poems.

stiLL, Life

From the graveyard everything looks good.
Shrouded, now, in white,
crystallized, I see that.
I also see carbonized snow
as a good thing.

Pardon my cynicism, my failure to acknowledge this
sooner. I'll get to the point.

How many of us ever take time to enjoy
the Earth's exquisite intricacies? Victorian lace.
Spiderwebs. The organza wing
of a common fly.

Who, among us, actually hears
bracelets in the chilly wind? A rattlesnake
coiling through light?

Put it this way.
Next time you claim to be bored,
visualize brownish-blackish grim nothingness
and then feed on the world,
one breath at a time. Imagine the tang
of unusual spices on your tongue;
red dust falling
lightly
from a powdered stamen.

Loosen the flower, drink some wine,
make your solemn declaration
singingly—

I can't even imagine not being here.

A WORD ABOUT SEDNA—GIVER AND TAKER OF LIFE

Sedna, the Sea Spirit, is one of the most respected and feared figures in Inuit mythology. Often depicted as a mermaid in Native carvings, she goes by over forty different names, including Nuliajuk ("young girl") and Takanaaluk ("Big Woman Down There"). It is difficult to pin down a definitive version of the story, since details of the myth vary from place to place.

In one variant, Sedna starts out as a beautiful girl living with her father by the seashore. Proud and somewhat spoiled, she rejects every suitor who comes her way. Intent on marrying her off, her exasperated father eventually forces her into a union with his lead dog. Before long, however, the dog-husband begins to show his true colours. Lazy and unproductive, he is unable to provide for his new wife. Sedna's father has him drowned.

Widowed, Sedna banishes her children from home. Those most human-like are cast out to sea and directed south (destined, according to the myth, to become the first White men); those most resembling dogs are pushed further out into the ocean, in the hope that they might learn to fish and hunt (slated to become the first Aboriginal peoples).

Sedna's second marriage is equally doomed: Duped by a storm bird disguised as a man, she ends up his hostage on a bleak and deserted island. When Sedna's father gets wind of her predicament, he paddles out on a rescue mission to save her. Cleverly, Sedna finds a way to elude her captor and is finally reunited with her father. The angry bird drums up a violent storm in revenge.

Fearing for his life, the father, for a second time, sacrifices his daughter—this time by casting her overboard. Scrambling to save herself, she clings to the gunwale, but her father smashes his paddle across her hands, severing her fingers at the joints. (Sucked underwater, they become the first seals, walruses, and whales of the North.)

In a final bid for survival, Sedna throws her elbows over the boat, but her father spears her in the eye with his oar. Fingerless and one-eyed, she ripples to the ocean floor, where she will spend eternity guarding the creatures born from her sunken digits.

Legend characterizes Sedna as vengeful and cruel, angry at Man for his evil deeds which manifest as body sores and as lice in her hair. Raging undersea, she conjures up storms to sabotage hunters. Those she deems worthy and respectful of life are granted the gift of food—a sea beast from her watery lair. The sinful others perish in starvation.

In lean times, shamans are sent on a difficult journey through the spirit world to appease Sedna and restore harmony on earth. Respectfully, they comb out her tangled hair, waiting for her wrath to subside.

200–

AGMV Marquis

MEMBER OF SCABRINI MEDIA

Quebec, Canada
2002